DATE DUE

American Lives

Jane
Addams

Elizabeth Raum

Heinemann Library
Chicago, Illinois

Designed by Heinemann Library
Photo research by Iris Wong and
Stephanie L. Miller
Printed in China by WKT Company Limited.

08 07 06 05 04
10 9 8 7 6 5 4 3 2 1

Library of Congress Cataloging-in-Publication Data
Raum, Elizabeth.
  Jane Addams / Elizabeth Raum.
      p. cm. -- (American lives (Heinemann Library
(Firm))) Summary: A biography of the social activist
known for founding Hull House in Chicago and for
winning the Nobel Peace Prize in 1931.
Includes bibliographical references and index.
  ISBN 1-4034-4992-9 (Hardcover) --
  ISBN 1-4034-5707-7 (Paperback)
 1. Addams, Jane, 1860-1935--Juvenile literature.
 2. Women social workers--United States--
Biography--Juvenile literature. 3. Women social
reformers--United States--Biography--Juvenile
literature. [1. Addams, Jane, 1860-1935. 2. Social
reformers. 3. Nobel Prizes--Biography. 4. Women--
Biography.] I. Title. II. Series.
  HV40.32.A33R38 2003
  361.92--dc22
                          2003015749

Acknowledgments
The author and publishers are grateful to the
following for permission to reproduce copyright
material: Icon, pp. 4-6, 8, 9, 13, 14, 16–18, 21–23,
27–29 Jane Addams Memorial Collection/University
of Illinois at Chicago; p. 7 Library of Congress;
pp. 10, 11, 19, 20, 25, 26 Jane Addams Collection/
Swarthmore College Peace Collection; p. 24
published in *Twenty Years at Hull-House*, The
Chautauqua Press, NY, 1910

Cover photograph by Jane Addams Memorial
Collection/The University Library/University
of Illinois at Chicago

The author would like to thank her editor,
Angela McHaney Brown, for her support
and encouragement.

The publisher would like to thank Michelle Rimsa
for her comments in the preparation of this book.

Every effort has been made to contact copyright
holders of any material reproduced in this book.
Any omissions will be rectified in subsequent
printings if notice is given to the publisher.

The cover image of Jane Addams was taken in 1914.
She was 54 years old.

Contents

Some words are shown in bold, **like this.** You can find out what they mean by looking in the glossary.

Ugly Duckling

Jennie Addams thought of herself as an ugly duckling. She was pigeon-toed, and her head tilted to one side because her spine was curved. More than anything else, she wanted to be like other children. But Jennie could not change the way she looked. She also could not stop caring about what other people said and did. Jennie wanted to make the world a more caring place.

This is a photo of Jennie taken in 1866. She was six years old.

This is the house where Jennie was born in Cedarville, Illinois.

Laura Jane Addams, who was called Jennie as a child, was born on September 6, 1860, in Cedarville, Illinois. When Jennie was only two years old, her mother, Sarah, died. Jennie's older brother and three older sisters helped take care of Jennie, but she spent most of her time with her father, John Huy Addams. Jennie loved and admired her father more than anyone else in the world.

The Open Door

Jennie's father owned a flour mill and a lumber mill. He used his money to help others. He built Cedarville's school and church. He invited friends and neighbors to borrow his books, turning his home into the town's first library. The front door to the Addams home was never locked. Many years later when Jane Addams had a home of her own, she always kept the doors unlocked and welcomed visits from her neighbors.

John Addams was a generous and caring man. He was a very good father to Jennie.

Mr. Addams shared his love of **history** with Jennie. Her favorite stories were about Abraham Lincoln, the President of the United States. He was a friend of her father's. One

This is the funeral procession in Washington, D.C., for President Abraham Lincoln.

of the saddest days of Jennie's childhood was the day President Lincoln was killed. Jennie would always remember seeing her father cry over the death of his friend.

Abraham Lincoln

Abraham Lincoln lived in Springfield, Illinois, where he served in the Illinois State **Legislature.** *Lincoln became the sixteenth president of the United States in 1861. He was killed in 1865 by John Wilkes Booth.*

Growing Up

When Jennie was six, she went to Freeport, Illinois, with her father on a business trip. They visited a poor area of the city. Jennie had never seen **poverty** before.

She asked her father why the people lived in such small, crowded houses. He told her that many people were not as lucky as she was. Her father helped Jennie understand that it was important for those who have enough to help those who do not.

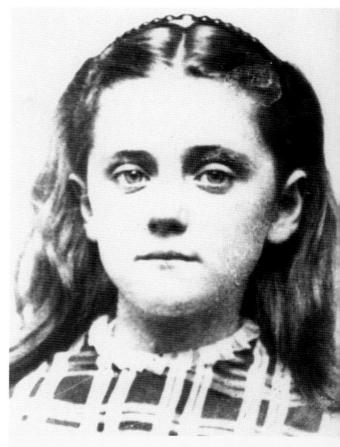

At age eight, Jennie already understood that many people were not as lucky as she was to have a good home and nice family.

This is a picture of Jennie at age sixteen with her stepmother, Anna, and stepbrother George.

Jennie's life changed when her father married Anna Haldeman in 1868. Anna had two children: Harry, who was eighteen, and George, who was six months younger than Jennie. Anna encouraged Jennie to play outdoors with George. Jennie, who had always been weak and sickly, grew strong and healthy from the exercise and fresh air. Anna taught Jennie good manners and read and sang songs with her. Anna helped Jennie gain more self-**confidence.**

9

College

Jennie loved reading. She was always a good student. Both John and Anna Addams believed that women should go to school. When Jennie, now called Jane, was sixteen, she wanted to go to Smith College in Massachusetts. Her father would not let her, however, because it was too far away.

In 1881 Jane became the first woman to earn a bachelor of arts degree from Rockford Female Seminary.

Instead Jane attended Rockford Female **Seminary,** as her three older sisters had done. It was in Rockford, Illinois, about 30 miles from her home in Cedarville. She got very good grades and made many friends.

The Life of Jane Addams

1860	1877	1889	1910
Born in Cedarville, Illinois, on September 6	*Attended Rockford Female Seminary*	*Opened Hull-House in Chicago*	*Wrote* Twenty Years at Hull-House

Jane became the best-known graduate of Rockford College, as the school is now known.

Jane joined the **debate team,** worked on the school magazine, and learned **taxidermy,** the art of stuffing and preserving a dead animal. She hoped to become a doctor.

Jane's Speech

In 1880 Jane gave a speech to the other students at Rockford. She said that a woman "wishes not to be a man, nor like a man, but she claims the same right to independent thought and action."

1915	**1931**	**1935**
Helped start the Woman's Peace Party	*Won Nobel Peace Prize*	*Died on May 21*

11

Time of Troubles

In 1881, when Jane was twenty, her father died. This made Jane feel lost and alone. Everything in Cedarville reminded Jane of her father, so she moved to Philadelphia, Pennsylvania. She attended the Woman's Medical College there. Jane did well in her studies, but she soon lost interest in becoming a doctor. She also began to have terrible pains in her back. After a back operation, she had to stay in bed for six months.

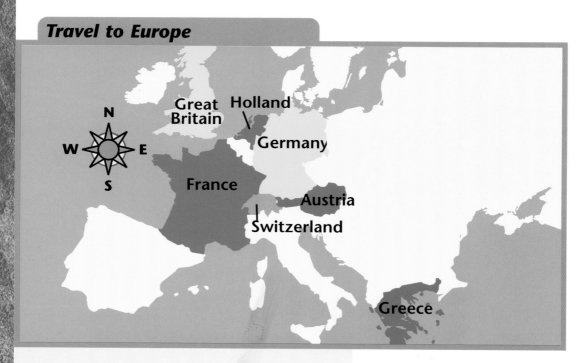

Travel to Europe

Great Britain

Holland

Germany

France

Austria

Switzerland

Greece

N W E S

Jane's trip to Europe helped her to recover from her operation.

Jane's doctor suggested that a trip to Europe would be restful. Jane and her stepmother spent nearly two years in Europe. They went to museums and art galleries and visited the homes of rich friends.

While in Europe, Jane saw poor people begging for food. She remembered visiting Freeport, Illinois, with her father and hearing him say that those who have a lot should help those who do not. Jane wanted to help, but she had no idea what she could do.

Puss Ellwood, Jane (center), and Mary Ellwood were good friends in Europe.

13

A New Purpose

Ellen Starr taught school for ten years before working with Jane.

In 1887, when Jane Addams was 27, she returned to Europe with her friends Ellen Starr and Sarah Anderson. In London, England, Jane and her friends visited Toynbee Hall, home to fifteen educated young men who lived among the poor people of London and tried to help their neighbors. Toynbee Hall was called a **settlement house** because the men settled in a poor part of the city. Jane decided to start her own settlement house in Chicago.

Jane's family told her it would be better if she got married and settled down to raise a family. Jane disagreed. She knew she could not work among the poor if she was caring for a husband and children of her own. Jane began raising money to build her settlement house. For several months, she spoke to women's groups and church groups. She was an excellent speaker, and she led many people to give money to the project.

Jane lived in a few different places before settling in Chicago, Illinois.

Settling in Chicago

N
W E
S

MAINE
VERMONT
NEW HAMPSHIRE
MASSACHUSETTS
RHODE ISLAND
CONNECTICUT
WISCONSIN
NEW YORK
MICHIGAN
Cedarville
Chicago
PENNSYLVANIA • New York
Philadelphia • NEW JERSEY
Freeport Rockford
Washington, D.C.
INDIANA OHIO
DELAWARE
ILLINOIS
MARYLAND
WEST
VIRGINIA
VIRGINIA
KENTUCKY
NORTH CAROLINA
TENNESSEE

Hull-House

Addams found a house at 335 South Halsted Street in Chicago where she could set up a settlement house. It was in the middle of a poor neighborhood, and it was big. The first floor was used as a **warehouse** and offices. Addams rented the second floor and a large room on the first floor. Within a year, she owned the whole house. She called it Hull-House in honor of its builder, Charles Hull.

Hull-House was a place where immigrants and poor people could get child care, English classes, and help finding work.

There were many immigrant families in the neighborhood surrounding Hull-House.

Most of the people who lived near Hull-House were **immigrants** who had come to the United States from Greece, Italy, Russia, Ireland, Poland, or Germany. Many did not speak English. They worked long hours to earn money for food and rent.

Some children had to work to help support their families. Other children, even babies, were left home alone. Addams knew life was difficult for them. She hoped Hull-House would be a place where they felt welcome.

Welcome

Addams and Ellen Starr spent hours fixing up the house. Addams brought over her best books, furniture, paintings, and silverware. Her family was sure her house would be robbed, but Addams planned to keep the doors open just as her father had kept an open door in Cedarville. In September 1889, when Addams was 29, she and Ellen moved into Hull-House. Addams put a big mat by the front door that said WELCOME.

People of all different backgrounds belonged to clubs at Hull-House. It became a popular meeting place.

Addams knew the time and effort she put into Hull-House would be worth it. It made her feel good to help others.

At first, her neighbors did not trust Addams. Why would a rich woman chose to live in their neighborhood? But Addams was determined to be a good neighbor. She invited some neighborhood women to tea. They came and enjoyed the warm welcome of Hull-House. Italian girls from a nearby factory were invited to supper. They decided to form a reading group.

Caring for Others

Addams started a kindergarten and a nursery to provide free daycare to poor working mothers who had no other place to leave their children. She fed the children, gave them baths, and read to them. Addams asked a local **landlord** to tear down some old buildings and to build a playground. It became the first public playground in Chicago. Addams also fought to change laws so children under age fourteen would not be allowed to work.

Addams helped give children in Chicago a safe place to play.

More and more young women came to Hull-House as settlement workers. There was enough space for 25 women to live there at one time. They helped pay the costs of running the house, worked in the nursery and kitchen, or taught classes.

Many women stayed only a short time, but others, like Ellen Starr and Mary Rozet Smith, stayed for years. Addams and the settlement workers rarely took vacations. There was too much important work for them to do.

Mary Rozet Smith became Addams's best friend and companion.

Building Pride

Within two years of opening, Hull-House had 1,000 visitors each week. By 1893, there were 2,000 visitors each week. Neighborhood women, children, and men visited Hull-House to attend book groups, **lectures,** musical events, plays, or daycare. Many languages were spoken at Hull-House so that everyone felt included. There were lectures in German and Russian and book groups in Italian.

When Addams learned that many **immigrants** had special skills, like weaving and sewing, she set up workshops for them. There the immigrants were able to continue to make beautiful things.

Children of immigrants were able to learn new skills, such as cooking, in the classes held at Hull-House.

"Lady Jane" was not afraid to speak out.

Addams hoped children would be proud of their parents. She wanted people to be proud of their neighborhood, too, but garbage was littering the streets. Addams's nephew could not visit her because his doctor believed the garbage in the streets would make him sick. Addams complained so much about the problem that the mayor made her garbage inspector. For several weeks, she followed garbage trucks to make sure the workers picked up the trash.

Hull-House Firsts

- *First settlement house in Chicago*
- *First public playground in Chicago*
- *First little theater in the United States*
- *First U.S. citizenship classes*
- *First free art exhibits in Chicago*
- *First public swimming pool in Chicago*
- *First Boy Scout troop in Chicago*

Writing and Speaking Out

Even though she was busy with Hull-House, Addams found time to write books and to speak to large audiences. She visited England and Russia in 1896. From 1905 to 1909 she was a member of the Chicago **School Board,** where she pushed for better schools. In 1910 she wrote her fourth book, *Twenty Years at Hull-House*. Everyone wanted to read it.

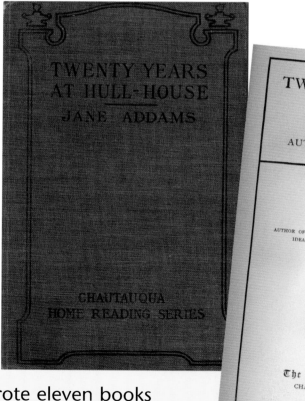

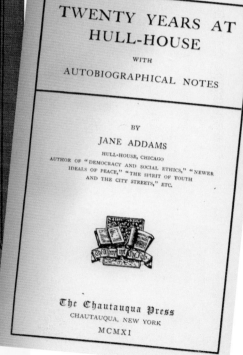

TWENTY YEARS AT
HULL-HOUSE

WITH

AUTOBIOGRAPHICAL NOTES

BY

JANE ADDAMS

HULL-HOUSE, CHICAGO
AUTHOR OF "DEMOCRACY AND SOCIAL ETHICS," "NEWER IDEALS OF PEACE," "THE SPIRIT OF YOUTH AND THE CITY STREETS," ETC.

The Chautauqua Press
CHAUTAUQUA, NEW YORK
MCMXI

Addams wrote eleven books about her experiences at Hull-House.

Addams cared about all people. She was one of the first members of the National Association for the Advancement of Colored People 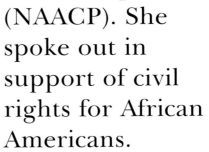 (NAACP). She spoke out in support of civil rights for African Americans.

Addams went on a train tour that made stops between Chicago and Springfield, Illinois. She spoke at every stop about suffrage.

At about the same time, she began speaking in favor of voting rights, or **suffrage,** for women. Her work at Hull-House had made her certain that women could change the world.

Women and Peace

In 1910 Addams wrote about giving women the vote in *The Ladies Home Journal.* Her **article** was read by thousands of women. Addams became one of the most important women in the United States. When she spoke, people listened. When she entered a room, people clapped. Her hard work at Hull-House had made her a hero. In 1911, she was elected vice president of the National American Woman **Suffrage** Association.

These women were selected to attend the First International Congress of Women in 1915.

Addams (right) and Mary McDowell marched for peace during World War I.

But when Addams spoke out against the war in Europe, many people turned against her. Not everyone shared her beliefs. In 1915 Addams visited Europe with other members of the Woman's Peace Party.

When she returned home, Addams gave speeches against the war. But in 1917, the United States sent soldiers to Europe. Addams was no longer invited to speak to groups.

Nobel Peace Prize

During the war, Addams continued her work at Hull-House. After the war ended, she traveled to Zurich, Switzerland, for a second women's peace conference. Many people were starving there, because farmers who were away fighting had not planted crops. Addams helped set up food drives to help people in Europe.

Addams loved working with children. Here she is shown reading to children at a nursery around 1930.

Thousands of people came to Hull-House to say goodbye at Addams's funeral in 1935.

In 1931 Addams became the second woman to be awarded the Nobel Peace Prize. This important award honored her work for peace. She received a peace medal and $16,480, which would be about $170,000 in today's dollars. She gave the money to the Women's International League for Peace and Freedom.

When she died of **cancer** on May 21, 1935, at age 74, thousands of people came to her funeral. Jane Addams had shown many people that the world could be a more caring place.

Glossary

article   report written in a magazine or newspaper

cancer   disease involving abnormal cells that replace normal cells

confidence   belief in one's own ability

debate team   group that argues with other groups about a set topic

gallery   place where art is shown

history   study of the past

immigrant   person who moves to a new country

independent   to do as you wish

landlord   person who rents land or houses to others

lecture   talk given before an audience

legislature   elected group of people who make the laws for a state or country

poverty   condition of being poor

school board   group of people who are in charge of the schools

seminary   private school for young women

settlement house   community center offering free services

suffrage   right to vote

taxidermy   art of stuffing and preserving a dead animal

warehouse   building where goods are stored

wealthy   rich

More Books to Read

Armentrout, David and Patricia. *Jane Addams.* Vero Beach, Fl.: Rourke, 2002.

Riley, John B. *Jane Addams.* Greensboro, N.C.: First Biographies, 2000.

Simon, Charman. *Jane Addams.* New York: Children's Press, 1998.

Places to Visit

Jane Addams Hull-House Museum
The University of Illinois at Chicago
800 S. Halsted
Chicago, Illinois 60607-7017
Visitor Information: (312) 413-5353

Cedarville Historical Museum
Cherry Street
Cedarville, Illinois
Visitor Information: (815) 563-4701
or (800) 369-2955

Stephenson County Historical Society
1440 South Carroll Avenue
Freeport, Illinois 61032
Visitor Information: (815) 232-8419

Index